Let it Burn

a poetry collection

Meagan Murtaugh

Cover Art by Ellie Meisner

DEDICATION

For me.

And for you reading this right now.
Because you deserve to be loved the right way.
Never forget that, okay?

ACKNOWLEDGMENTS

Those who I love, know that I love them.

To my parents; Mom, Nick, Daddy, Donna.
To my siblings; Harry Jr., Kayla, Nick Jr., Emily, Dakota
To my dog; Jax.
To my dear friends; both old and new.
To my readers, who made "Moomer Poetry" a thing.

Thank you for supporting me in telling my story through poetry…

I love you more than all the sunsets I will forever chase in the sky.

To my fellow survivors: I see you. I am so proud of you.

Love,

"Moomer"

Ps. To my Grampap Harry, who in tough times has always told me,
"never forget who you are."
Thank you. I love you. I won't.
I promise.

Prelude

And when this is finally over,
I promise,
I won't look back.

> You'll become the **dust**
> that floats behind me
> when I walk towards him.

You'll be the bridge
I lit on fire & let **burn**
when I finally crossed over.

> You'll be the **ashes** of my past...

STILL BURNING

I used to tell him that I loved the way his hands felt.
The way they would grab my face
and interlock with my fingers.
His hands.
I became so afraid of what once
was my favorite part of him.

I sacrificed myself
little by little,
without even realizing
that I was slowly breaking
& losing who I was in the process.

I was already gone, before I had even left.
       My soul was floating,
but my body stayed in your shadows.
…Always in your shadows.
Like unimportant mail that you toss in a junk drawer.
      "I'll get to it," you'd say.

          I'll get to you, one day.

His love was like the ocean
when the water crashes onto the sand.
It would give me what I wanted,
and then quickly take it away without warning.

*extended version of poem in same chapter, "Still Burning," on page 76.

All we long for,
is for someone to take the
broken pieces of our past
and mold them into something more
beautiful.

Red wine stains & traces of blame
edge the corners of my lips.
Messy hair & word out words.
My body. Tired.
My face. Always looking blank.
My mind. Screaming.
It's like you always had this imaginary black tape
covering my mouth.

Caged, he keeps me.
Clipped wings and steel bars.
He keeps me.
Suffocated by the fear,
that I'll never be able to break free.
Just when my toes lift off the ground,
he always pulls my chains back down.

Each scar became a reminder
of another day gone by.
I laid there
acting like it's normal
to be kissed by bruises
while my heart confuses
the difference
between heaven and hell.

I've been in love with someone
who didn't know how to love me back.
I've been loved by someone
who I couldn't let love me.

I don't know which is worse.

To be broken.
Or to break.

I was young and bored.
I was twenty-five and half alive.
I craved something new.
I begged for a thrill.
He gave me that,
but with a side of darkness
that was hidden underneath his crisp shirts,
charming smile
and infectious laugh.

Each time he'd tell a lie,
a compliment immediately followed.
Each time he'd kiss my forehead,
a bruise appeared months later.

I never noticed the strings that dangled from my shoulders.

Like a marionette,
I just wanted to abide.

His love was something I never knew existed.
His love came at a cost.

His love was never mine.

His love.
Was his.

What he'll never realize,
is how strong I was for him
when I could barely hold my own weight.

I was a tree standing alone
with my roots barely grasping the surface.
And he was the storm that I couldn't avoid
from ripping me out of the ground.

But why did you stay?
You don't understand.

He made my world feel so small,
that I couldn't see the exit.

I settled.
For the first one who said he saw the stars in my eyes.
I laid my armor at his feet.
I held out my hands to be tied.
I looked blindly
at a blank page while someone else wrote my story…

*poem ends in Chapter 2; "Ashes," page 92.

My life was made of equal parts.
Flowers & fires.
Black & blues.
Salt & honey.
You & You.

Let it Burn

In loving you,
I fed the fire.
I fed your fire with all the good things
I knew would help keep you visible,
but slowly make me melt away.

All the best parts of me.
Tossed in the flames,
knowing they'd just turn to smoke
and drift further away.

I continued to feed the fire,
And it did nothing but burn me.

He lived in a world with no mirrors.
If he looked at himself,
he would shatter.

He lived for the snow.
He'd make angels by himself,
until they'd melt away
and he was left with nothing.

I was Summer, Spring and Fall.
And every single time,
he chose Winter.

I felt shame…
For taking up so much space
in my own head,
when you reserved nothing in yours for me.

I felt guilt…
For taking up so much time
in my life,
when you didn't factor me into yours…

*Poem ends in Chapter 3, "Dust," page 139.

You said you'd always cover me,
But when the rain came,
I felt it beat hard on my back.
It became clear that you only showed up when
the sun came.

I forced myself
to count all the daggers you left in my back.
Ten.
Maybe more.
I can't remember them all.
In fact, I probably blocked a lot of them out.

I just know that each one left a different scar.
A different story.
A different apology.
A different excuse to stay again.

Another reason to pretend they weren't ever there.

Except they were.

I keep asking myself...
When will they be set free with me?

First,
he showed me how well he could love me.
He set me up for a feeling
that I thought would change my world in an instant.

So, I went inside my safe.
A place not even I had been before.
I handed him the keys to my heart.

I let go.

He showed me how well he could love me.
And then he didn't.

I once loved someone so much,
that I tried to put their puzzle back together.
Little by little.
Day by day.

And all he did
was continue to misplace
pieces of mine.

He promised me the world
and I believed it
every time.

I saw everything for what I wanted it to be.
Instead of seeing what it truly was.

I always made hearts out of scars.

I hate what you took from me.
A piece of me that was special.
A part of me that was only reserved for
"him."
You never were "him."

You watched me crumble,
and then you swept the mess away.

Love.
He throws it around like a tether ball.
Whoever it hits,
it just continues to wrap around their beautiful soul
until they have nothing left,

but him.

That word to him is nothing more
than an entrance into someone else's perfect world.
In preparation
to burn it all down.

My angel eyes
tried to see past the devil in you.
You trapped me.
Like a maze with no exits.

My insides were empty.
Faking smiles on days I wanted to scream.

Leaving tears on brand new pillowcases
while you stood 3 feet away
and watched me drown myself.

He was always seeing red.
He turned daisies into dandelions.
And I stood there quietly,
with my hands tied behind my back
watching them wilt with me.

He smoked me like a cigarette,
and then refused to exhale.
I waited.
For so long I waited for him to breathe for me,
and he never could.

I'd catch myself walking through the dark,
and still I'd stay.
I couldn't see for miles
and it felt like a life sentence.
Rose colored glasses
and scars hidden behind crooked smiles.

I poured all my sunshine into one person,

and they refused to see me as their sky.

I didn't realize
that I had dug a grave for myself
the moment I told you

that I needed you.

Jaw always clenched.
Eyes constantly wide open.
My body became numb.
The actions became routine.

Alert at all times
just waiting to make my next mistake.

Every time I was holding on,
I felt my fingers tense up.
My grip slowly trying to let go.

I'd beg to grab the air…

But you would never let me.

The problem was
that he devoured me with his words.
They could cradle me like a newborn baby,
or slice right through me like a just sharpened blade.

He never could admit
that I was the song people play on repeat.
The one they turn up to eleven
with their windows down on the highway.
I was the lyrics that lingered on his brain.
The ones that made him think so hard,
he would rather sit in silence instead.

You are just like
the moon and the sun.
You disappear when it doesn't feel right.
Then think you can just come back,

and screw up all my plans.

My heart
will always be
a half a beat between
the way you made me feel
and the way I should have felt
the entire time
you were abusing it.

Misery only lingers
on those who choose not to see
the beauty in anyone
other than themselves.

The room is quiet,
but my thoughts are loud.
My mind scatters,
and it's lost in the wild of my imagination.
I've been waiting so long to exhale,
and for some reason I can't.

With each breath in,
I fight so hard to let go…

*Poem ends in Chapter 3, "Dust," page 150.

He was the type of guy
who could have been given
the earth,
the stars,
the moon,
and the sun
all in one breath...

and he still would have asked for an umbrella.

The amount of times
I've asked "why"
could separate the cracks in the sky
for a lifetime.

The most bittersweet lesson in life is this:

At least one in your life
you will love someone.

And you will learn
what
love isn't.

I can feel.
Or I don't.
And that's fine.
For now.

But one day,
I will.

And will mean something.

Everything.

You were my favorite escape
until you made me get lost.
I'd search for you in every corner,
and all I was left with

was a bunch of open space.

You were the type of person
who would put a band aid
over a knife wound,
and casually ask if I was okay.

I wasn't.

He races through life.
Never allowing himself to grieve
or wallow in his own mistakes.
He burns through every moment,
just as quickly as he burned through me...

*Poem ends in Chapter 3, "Dust," page 166.

The hardest part for me,
was seeing two lives
right in front of my face,
and finally choosing the one
that I was always afraid to choose.

If only his truths were the only things able to be spoken by him.
His world would be so quiet.

We would be able to hear the stars die
when they shoot down from the sky.

You can pretend all you want.
And let lies spit like wildfire from your broken lips.
Your eyes hold the movie clips
of that night.
And I know they play on repeat when you're alone.

I know they tell a different story than the one you tell.

The thing was…
I knew you had to go
when all my dreams
became all about you.

And you just let me go on with my life
like it was normal to stop dreaming for me.

The way the water reflects off her eyes,
tells me a story of beautiful pain.

It reminded me of you,
and how you loved the color red.
You'd lock me inside,
and I'd listen because the outside was pretty.

Then when I'd enter,
you'd watch me fall apart in silence.

You'd watch the crimson drops
get stuck in the corners of my lips.

I've been in a daze
the last few days…
Just wanting all of this to fade away.

I watched him
make wishes on shooting stars
and dandelions,
while I stood there never knowing
if I was enough.

I wrote your name in the sand,
and watched the waves swallow you whole.

I searched for pearls in your eyes,
and all I found were empty shells.

She'll change for him.
She'll completely erase the parts of herself
that make her,
her.
Just to fit the mold that he tells her
is his definition of a perfect love.

First the hair.
Then the clothes.
Next, her voice.

He'll take that all away,
until all she has left is,

Him.

You are just like the sky when it turns to grey.
You cover me with dark clouds.
You bring the rain.

When you'd hurt,
I'd rush to your side.
When I'd hurt,
you'd hide.

He made my world blurry.
His eyes told lies
and then they rolled off his tongue
like it was easy.
Each and every time.
Practiced and rehearsed
in his head,
likes he's done this many times before.

One day you will break.
Like glass you will shatter.
And don't worry.
She'll figure out exactly who you are.
And I'll laugh.
because your life is a sad movie,
and sweetheart,
you're the star.

I went to a lot of places with you,
and none of them felt like home.

So, I started to wonder
if I was just better off alone…

*Poem ends in Chapter 3, "Dust," page 174.

He could only give her a world
in black and white.
And all she wanted
was a life in color.

Like deep water,
she was silent.
His lips tasted of salt.
He was both addicting and bitter
all at once.

Love today.
Gone tomorrow.
Now you pass each other
like strangers on a busy street.

He was a lot like the moon.
He shined bright
and was admired when he was full.
But always disappeared when a storm came.

Shattered pieces of smashed mirror
scattered across the floor.
She crawled through broken glass
just to get away from you,
and see her new reflection.

I always moved the lines you crossed.
You broke me down
until I felt lost.
I'd lock the bedroom door and scream,
writing pages in my journal,
trying to justify that this was nothing but a bad dream.

I was walking through fire
most of the time.
The best pieces of me would burn
and I'd always let you put band aids
over the wounds…

*Poem ends in Chapter 2, "Ashes," page 100.

Sweetheart,

Always watch his eyes
when he's telling you a story.

They'll pierce right through you.
They'll break your soul in pieces.

I wonder how much smoke
you've choked on from all the bridges you've burned.
I'd probably have to walk through fog
just to get a clear picture
of your crooked face again.

Darling,

He loves you the way he loved me.
And the one before me.
And just like the ocean,
when the waves crash up against the shore…
He gives
until it's too much for him.

Then he quickly takes it all away
without warning.

He'll leave you
washed up on the sand.
And you'll be standing there for days
never knowing if you're enough.

Until the next wave comes
and knocks you down again.

It used to echo in my head.
Over and over.
The pounding sound of his beating drum.
The only tune he'd ever march to.
The only one that mattered to him.

And it broke me.

Because it resembled by heart
every time he'd play with it.

You always knew just what to say.
The way you'd change
from night to day.
You'd strike a chord on my soul
and then you'd watch me melt away.

ASHES

Something changed in me that day.
I walked to the quietest part of the desert.
Both hesitant and full of wonder.
I heard nothing.
And that was when I felt everything.

I'm not there yet.
I still can't feel anything deeper than my skin.
I laugh at those who cry
because I constantly wonder why.
Why can't I cry?

Then I give myself some grace.
I remember where I've been.

Since I woke up from this life
that he made me believe was meant for me,
I find myself becoming the person I really am.

When you are finally set free,
so is the person they
trained you to be.

And.
So.
I made the choice.

I flew away.

It sucked me up
and placed me in the center of the universe.
Had me watch from up above
and so, I held my breath
until I fell completely out of love.
I was asphyxiated by the sky.
and now I know why.

He found me when I was six feet under water
and dragged me to the surface
while I gasped for air.

It was the first time in years I could feel myself breathe.

When these nights start getting cold
and you need someone to hold,
it will be me who you're searching for.

But I won't be there anymore.

I went to the ends of the earth
and back for you.

And you still reminded me that you never asked me to.

The bridge that went
from me to you
is engulfed in flames.

You lit the match.
I just finally to decided
to let it burn.

Let the ashes fill the air
and drift away with you.

Drown out the sounds.
Kick the pavement until my soles burn.
Not sure how long it'll be
until I need a hand to hold.
Being intertwined in someone else's something.

He's the mountain.
And I'm just a girl afraid to climb it.
But there are rocks to hold onto
And ledges to scale.

At the top there's a sunset I've never seen before.

I'm jealous of the sky
& it's ability to just let it all go.

I'm like an untouched puzzle,
just scattered into thousands of pieces.
And I need to be in a place,
where even if all the pieces don't fit,
or some are missing,
that I can still be put together,
and feel complete.

I'm starting to notice,
that most of the important things I know,
I learned by falling.

The ground teaches me.

It teaches me more than the sky
and stars ever could.

I lay back.
My body pressed against the concrete floor,
staring up at the sun.
It's blinding.
Kind of like my love for you was.

*Continued from page 17.

(...I settled.
For the first one who said he saw the stars in my eyes.
I laid my armor at his feet.
I held out my hands to be tied.
I looked blindly
at a blank page while someone else wrote my story...)

The ink was never permanent.
Those pages have been ripped.
Tossed away.
I tossed them all away
with all the other over fabricated words you spoke.

Let it Burn

I let him break me like glass.
My colorful heart
lay shattered on the floor.

A stained glassed window
just waiting to be put together
and be a beautiful work of art instead.

I crave the kind of love
that lives in black and white photos.
The kind where you see stars in the daylight.

When you start to become thankful
for the pain,
that's when it suddenly
all starts to melt away.

I remember the day I learned how to swim again.
I was in the middle of an ocean.
Surrounded by a thunderstorm.
I was drowning,
but a small part of me was able to stay above water.

And in the midst of gasping for air,
I taught myself to float.

I still look back sometimes.
Thinking about all of crimes
I let go of when you were mine.

Questions I know will never be answered
race through my brain
like a permanent stain
left in the back of my mind
when you were mine.

You never really were mine.

Things fall apart.
They break.
They shatter.
They get lost in another universe.

So, when my things fell apart.
I fell apart, too.

When my things broke,
I broke, too.

When my things shattered,
I shattered, too.

I got lost in another universe with all those things
and felt myself look for a way to be fixed.

When my things started to get fixed,
I was fixed, too.

I didn't know it at the time,
but I was searching for forever
in a temporary place.

My mind was lost in empty space.
My body was limp.
You never cared to see the pain that poured from my lifeless face.

*Continued from page 73.

(…I was walking through fire
most of the time.
The best pieces of me would burn
and I'd always let you put band aids
over the wounds…)

Then one day,
the rain came pouring down.
And washed it all away.
I watched you disappear.
I watched you drown.

And finally,
I didn't try to save you.

I let you go.

You took a lot from me.
But not the sunsets.
Their beauty runs through my veins.
Turning my blood different shades of color as the day passes me by.

The pink and orange setting fire
on my soul
from miles away.

They kept me alive
on days I just wanted to bury myself beneath the earth's surface.

The sunsets.
Those were almost mine.

She bottles up the clouds in her mind
and remembers them on a lonely day.
Trying to justify,
it's not always going to be this way.

I remember the days I prayed for you to wake up.
I'd lay hunched over in our bed,
while you sat up staring at the TV
in the other room.

Your eyes glazed over.
Your mind full of rage.
And I'd fall asleep,
just hoping you'd wake up next to me.

I remember the days I prayed for you.

Now I pray to forget you.

My story isn't one for the fairytales.
It's messy.
And scary.
And full of chaos.

I'd like to think it ends with
warm bodies
and calm souls

and me telling it.

And then she brushed her hair away
from the side of her face,
looked me right in the eyes,
her body shaking,
and she said:

"I'm not afraid of finding new love.
I'm afraid of feeling old pain."

I watched her lipstick smear.
I saw her mascara run.
I stood right in front of her while her body shook.

And then I broke the mirror
and threw the past in the trash.

Last night
I was outside in the cool breeze.
Sitting alone.

I had forgotten how the moon still shines
even when it's not whole.

She was born an ember.

And decided to throw all the
messy
complicated
screwed up
chapters of her life
in with the ashes.

And then she became the flame.

And some days,
all she needs
is to lay beneath the crescent moon

and let the Earth hold her.

I forced myself to stay awake
through all the pain.
My heart would earthquake
through the heavy rain.

Was told I had to feel it all
in order to let go of you.

I let my body hit the wall
and watched as you faded into the deep blue.

Some days,
I feel like I'm wired differently.
And other days
it seems like the lights won't turn on inside.

So, I sit here with the lights off.

Wondering when I'll finally
see clearly in the dark again.

It took every bone in my
tired, broken, and bruised body

to walk away from you.

I felt crippled.
My back colored in shades of black and blue.

I felt lost.
My heart knowing you were never true.

But it was time.
My soul finally knew.

I finally realized
that the universe was trying to tell me a story.

My story.

And instead of trying to turn the pages early,
I let myself lose control.

I started to understand
while I gazed at the sun setting before me,
that he took away the moments,
that now take my breath away.

And so, I poured out the rest of you.
The remainder of what still lived inside my heart,
but died in my soul.
I took a glass
that was already close to empty,
and let the last drops of you
completely dry out
along with every tear I ever shed.

How long will it be?
Before I start to see the stars align around us.
Before our worlds collide
at the exact moment it's meant to.
Before I'm your first thought in the morning
and your last thought at night.

Maybe when the air turns colder.
Maybe when the days get darker.
Maybe when I snap back to reality.

Or maybe it'll only be when I slowly drift away.

Dear You,

"I am deeply sorry."
I am deeply sorry
that you will always be you.
That you never cared to know the real me.
That thoughts of you now make me laugh.
But with pity.

"I am deeply sorry."
I am deeply sorry
that I realized how much better
my soul is without you.
That I radiate light when I walk into a room alone.
That others see what was holding me down all along.

"I am deeply sorry."
I am deeply sorry
that was you.

The problem is
that time never stops.
So here I am,
still waiting.
Still thinking of you.
Watching the sun rise and set with each passing day.
Wondering when you'll realize,
that I think of you.
And you'll think of me, too.

Love today.
Gone tomorrow.
Now you pass each other
like strangers on a busy street.

I remember counting every step
As you climbed the stairs.
Tightly closed my eyes tried to
imagine another place.
One where I wake up brand new.
And you're gone.
And he's here.

He's trying to lay next to me,
But I'm scared.
(And it's all your fault).

I close my eyes again.
My mind is aching to let him in.

I'm falling slow.
Just like the very first snow.

And then I melt into him.

I can see your heart beating through your chest.
But I can't feel a thing.
Am I here?
Or am I lost again.

The moon shines bright against your skin.
but there is no shadow for me to follow.

I'm left here on pause.
My heart dangling in the air.
Not sure when I should speak.
Feeling like I can't breathe too heavy,
or I'll break.
I already know the answer to the questions
I don't want to ask.

I guess I'm just wishing for this storm to pass.

I've been feeling the grip
loosen between the cracks in our fingers.
I think I'm letting go.
Because I don't think you can hold on anymore.
It's been keeping me up at night.
My dreams have turned to dust.
It's coming down on me like pouring rain.
I feel myself breaking down again.

I always felt the weight of you on my mind.
The way you'd echo in the dark,
you made me become blind.
I'd silence myself
every night
just to avoid an inevitable fight.

When his lips say one thing,
but your mind is telling you another.
Stuck between wanting this moment
to last
and wondering if you're wasting time.
So, you breathe in the clouds,
and just let go of time.

Just look at me.
Look at me the way you look at the sky
when it turns those bright shades
of purple and orange.
And everything else will fall into place.

They'll fall
just as beautiful as the sun does
on all those nights
you sit back and admire it.

I watched him deceive you.
I saw a few come and go.
And still
you went back for more.

I finally feel it all.
I used to be you.
Blind and afraid.
until I finally realized,
you can't change a man
who has no core.

I remember.
I remember always going back
to what continued to break me.
My body would ache
from the inside out
as I tried to justify the lasting pain.

Eyes always closed.
In a dark room with nowhere to go.

Until the sun left a beam
of light on my face one day.

If only he would look at me.
Look at me
the way I look at
poetry.

Sometimes the sun sets,
but it's too foggy out to see.
Your mind is racing.
Wondering.
Not knowing when your soul
will be set free.

You've been here before.
You've climbed every wall.

"Such is life."

You've said it countless times.

You've justified every fall.

She's afraid
of falling to pieces again.
So, I tell her how
we weren't put on this earth
to be delicate.

It's okay to bend sometimes.

You might even break.

You could have been.
You could have been
my pink sky,
my first snow,
my favorite view.

You could have been
that smell after it rains
when the earth kisses the sun.

Your heart's not afraid to break.
You stop overthinking
every word she says.

You'd slowly trace the outlines
of her skin with your fingertips.

Because in another lifetime,
you'd let yourself fall
for her.

I was just another story
in his little black book
that he'd share one day.

He'd wrap me in old newspaper
and toss me away.

His apology
sounds a lot like
trees in the back of a run-down forest.

Silent and forgotten.

The rain came down harder than ever before.
So, I asked myself if this was a sign.

Do I embrace the weight of my storms?
Or should I keep running towards the sun?

Let these dark clouds pass me by,
or fall back and touch the sky.

DUST

I wrote my old life on a piece of paper
and read it a few times.
As tears filled my eyes,
I knew it wasn't mine anymore.

So, I crumpled up my past,
and left it behind me.

*Continued from page 22.

(I felt shame…
For taking up so much space
In my own head,
When you reserved nothing in yours for me.

I felt guilt…
For taking up so much time
In my life,
When you didn't factor me into yours…)

I felt free…
When I finally let myself go
without your permission.

Pink skies
and sky lines.
Deep breaths
and crooked smiles.
Staring into space
while your eyes followed mine.

I'm not quite sure what we were looking at.
But it was the first time in a while I looked forward.

I watched her tilt her head back,
and open her arms up to the sky.
It was as if she was letting go
all at once.

And I got to witness her triumph
in silence.

He leaned in with grace
and I'm sure I smelled like fear.
I'm sure I looked worried
without even meaning to.
And then I felt his soul radiate
from his smile.

I finally exhaled.
I let myself go.

And so instead of dwelling on you,
I decided to take in the beauty of the earth
that I had forgotten surrounded me.

The never-ending miracles
that you allowed to pass me by
are now the things that make me feel whole again.

I remember trying to look so far ahead
and seeing nothing.
Just blank space filled with
unanswered questions.

So, I stayed in your shadows.

It took so long to see the sun
finally set before my eyes.

And once it did,
I was changed.

And you were gone.

The beautiful yet chaotic
irony of it all is that;
because of you,
I lost myself,
and yet,
because of you,

I found myself.

She laid with her head back
feeling ever present.
Just her and this moment.
Her mind at ease,
admiring the breeze
that freed her soul.

He was the fire
that crippled my bones…

And you were the one
who showed up out of nowhere,
and carried me home.

She was someone who still believed
that she could love
with a shattered heart.

And that made her remarkable.

We make wishes
on what we think are shooting stars,
while tiny bits of dust die right in front of us.
and still, we close our eyes
and hope for a miracle.

I think that's beautiful.

*Continued from page 44.

(The room is quiet,
but my thoughts are loud.
My mind scatters,
and it's lost in the wild of my imagination.
I've been waiting so long to exhale,
and for some reason I can't.

With each breath in,
I fight so hard to let go…)

**But finally,
I do.**

And my chest breaks in relief.

It's over.

The irony of it all,
was that you were the one
who stole the stars from my eyes.
Who took the light from my soul.
Who burned a hole where I was whole.

And now you are the one
left sitting in the dark.

It was just me and your stars.
I lied face up
admiring the dust that lit up around us.

Tracing your constellations
with the tips of my fingers.

In a world full of color,
I long to live in black and white.

Where old love exists
and the photos tell us stories
we can only remember
with the purest of hearts.

(…as I stare at a picture of my Grandparents when they were young).

What's so poetically beautiful about my world now,

is that it's finally
mine.

I remember when you were my love story.
And now you're my story of survival.

How sweet is it?
That I got to experience both.

That my heart is capable of so much,
and yours will never be enough.

He looked over at me
as if I had just hand painted the sky.
And I thought,
how wonderful is it,
to be thought of as someone who
brings sunsets to another person's eyes,
simply by showing up.

We have to squint when we open the shades.
The sun is so bright,
it makes our new the floors glisten.

The room smells like a combination of fresh paint
and white daisies.
The kind I'd pick up at the corner store
on my walk home from the dog park with Jax.

There's a coffee stain from morning
where a coaster should have been,
but I shake my head and smile,
because you came through the door with that dessert I love.
The place that's out of the way
on your drive home from work.

We skip dinner
and spend the night on the back patio.
Under a weighted blanket.
Our bodies intertwined.

I'm homesick.
For a place I can't wait to go one day.

I looked around at all the people.
I knew no one and it was okay.
I felt the breeze run through my hair.
I let my eyes get lost.
Never wanting to be found.

(Spain, the trip that changed my life):

I realized
that in order to find myself,
I had to go somewhere completely
alone.
Some place where I was new
and could see my old world
from a different view.

He's the fire in my bones.
The smell before the rain comes.
The wind you feel on the back of your neck
just before the seasons change.

The kind of man that makes you love thunderstorms again.

My mind went numb.
And with one subtle breath,
all of my past troubles just floated away
in the calm water
where my soul now rests.

I looked down below,
and finally felt my heart
match the flow of the ocean.

And so, I made a new plan.
Except it wasn't a plan at all.
Because the sun took me further
then I ever would have gone.
And up on the hill tops,
I started to see,
that this whole other world,
has always been waiting for me.

I fell back and touched the sky.
I floated above myself
and the clouds swallowed me whole.

In that moment,
I lost everything holding me down.

I was weightless.

She's got that glow about her now.

The kind that says,
"she's been through some dark pain,
but she's lighting her own way again."

Everything was crumbling.
Some things even turned to dust.
The world was turning
and I was standing still.

You pushed me off the edge,
and instead of crashing into the ground,
I levitated into the universe.

I disappeared before your eyes.

*Continued from page 51.

(He races through life.
Never allowing himself to grieve
or wallow in his own mistakes.
He burns through every moment,
just as quickly as he burned through me…)

But I…
I see the beauty in taking things in.
The way the rain falls.
The sky when it rises.
The colors of the leaves when they change
from season to season.

The way I've changed from season to season.

He held me back.
From all the things that would
eventually fill my soul.

So, I learned on my own,
to pour the sun, moon, and stars
into my life again.

I let the world take hold of me,
and watched in slow motion
as everything collided together
to make a beautiful cosmic explosion,
that lifted me to a better place.

The place where I belonged.

I left.
I left with the hope of returning to a new view.
One that didn't blind me
when I opened my eye lids on an early morning.

One that didn't cause me to
shut the shades
and not breathe in the crisp air that my lungs deserved.

I left.
I left with the hope of returning to a new life.
One that enriched my soul
and placed me in an eternal sunset.

I realized.
I wasn't just waiting for the end,
but the end was waiting for me.

The moon was always full
and I still tried to find a reason to stay and stare at it.
To find meaning in a mystical object,
that in the end,
meant nothing.

I broke free when he broke me
for the last time.

My heart no longer orbits around you.

She decided to name the stars.
And as each one fell from the night sky,
her body got warmer.
Her heart opened.

While her world was busy falling apart,
I watched her create a life
so beautiful
and pure
and new,
that even the darkest storm of her existence
somehow looked majestic.

Her hearts been bruised.
Her mind has, too.
But she finds comfort in his eyes.
Scared to lose control.
Afraid of what she'll find.
So, he draws a map of his soul.

And just like the leaves in the Fall,
she fell, too.

And it changed her.

And it was wonderful.

*Continued from page 66.

(I went to a lot of places with you,
and none of them felt like home.

So, I started to wonder
if I was just better off alone...)

But then I met a lot of people,
who really made me see,
that this whole time
for all my life
you were the only one
who couldn't love the real me.

He sees past my shell.
Slowly cracking it open.
Like when the usually closed shades
let in a glimmer of light in the mornings.
The kind of sun that gets you out of bed on a Monday.

You crashed into me like a wave.
I fell beneath the surface and
drowned in your eyes.
I couldn't help but hold onto you.
As you pulled me closer,
I felt comfort in your soul.
My body lost its shape.
I think I like it here.
Weightless together.
You made me lose all control.

I went to a place.
A place where I could breathe again.
I leaped without a parachute
into an open world.

I let go of everything,
and found myself waiting.

I am ready to be with someone
who will lay with me under a crescent moon,
and quietly watch our worlds collide.

When he took my hand,
I felt apart of me give in.
Like when you get caught in the rain
on a beautiful Spring afternoon.
You just let yourself stand beneath
the open sky.

You stay.

I decided it was time.
I took off the chains.
They were leaving indents on my heart.

I tossed them behind me,
and ran towards him.

The one before you
held my heart like it was made of glass.
And he loved to break things.

So, when I see you
hold my heart like it's made of star dust,
I can't help but believe in magic again.

She finally lived in a world with no fears.
She walked on a tightrope with no net.

And she was as graceful as ever.

I gave my all.
And you gave up.
I was breaking down
when I finally realized
that even giving you everything
would never be enough.

So, I let my body fall back.
I finally survived the inevitable car crash.

I always admire
the way the leaves fall
when the seasons change.

It reminds me how easy it can be to
let
things
go.

And start from scratch.

Today I decided
to let the sky open up on my face,
and exhale the leftover drops of pain
still lingering on my heart.

I always imagine
"home"
being something simple…
Our two half-filled coffee mugs
still sitting on the counter,
because you pulled me close to you,
and the rush your lips give me
is stronger than caffeine.

Because next to you,
I can see new life bloom.
And by your side,
I can feel both our worlds collide.

It's 6pm.
We've been sitting here for hours
just waiting for the sunset.
And I don't want to miss it.
I don't want to blink.
Because I just want to remember
the way you looked at me that night
when the sun went down.

And just like that,
the echo of your memory
has turned to dust.
The once familiar sound
is now forgotten.
The air feels safe to breathe again.

I know I'm the only one
who could make you feel like home.
I put the sun in your world
when it was nothing but clouds of grey.

So, when you let me leave,
I didn't hesitate this time.

I know you still obsess
over every single word I say.

I'll always and forever,
be the one that got away.

I remember thinking my world had ended.
My mind had turned to fog.
Until I stepped outside one night
into the dark.
The breeze made me feel alive again.
I felt a wave of new air
brush the bones in my cheeks.
And the light from the stars.
They took ahold of me.
They gave me a new purpose.

If I had only loved you
with half of my heart,
then I wouldn't have found myself
after you tore it apart.

I see stars in his eyes
when I close mine.
And I'm crossing my fingers
just wishing on them
that these constellations of dreams never end.

I watched her glance at her face
as she walked past the mirror.
Beaming with pride
because she finally lived in a world
with no fear.

Her body was floating.
Her hair effortlessly flowing.

And I finally was able to see.
This girl.
Was free.

And finally.
My mind runs clear.
Like a wave just brushed away
all the sandcastles we ever built.

Now I walk.
With fresh feet on the ground.
I feel the earth
between the cracks of my toes.
The water rising beneath me.

And then I see you drift away
with all those things
that I thought mattered.
But never did.

My eyes look towards the sun.
And a smile perks through my lip.
It's as if I've been trying to show my teeth for years.

The light from above.
It's leading me home.

You were always like a sandcastle.
Complicated and cliché.

But this just reminded me
why sandcastles,
they always eventually wash away.

My skin and bones.
They broke for you.

My heart and soul.
They healed for me.

If the sky's about to fall
and I end up losing it all,
I'll remember your face
and how it brought me to a better place.
I'll think back to how I memorized
that special light that shines in your eyes.

Right before the world ends,
you'll be the reason my heart mends.

With broken hands,
she held on again.
With broken hands,
she turns the page
and watched the words of her past melt away.

Her eyes have dried,
and have been opened wide.
And there's new leaves in November,
and it makes her remember
that since that perfect September,
she's new, too.

I don't want to ever forget
the way that it felt
to be held by the sun
when I was ten feet under ground
and almost freezing to death.

In your arms,
I feel my heart give in.
Don't break me.
Just take me.
Because I can feel myself
falling into
the deepest part of you.

I took a different way this time.
A road paved with unanswered questions.
But still I went.
And it led me to you.

I fell unexpectedly.
Just like the very first snow of Winter.
My hands cold on your face
as your fingers outline and trace
the melting snowflakes on my heart.

I waited so long to see
if there was an answer
in the heart that set me free.

I was broken with him.
Sometimes it would bring me to my knees.

I went to look for someone
to throw off my gravity,
screw with my reality,
take me to my destiny.

You and I collided.
Stopped trying to fight it.

Finally decided to let myself get lost in you.

I went through all the phases.
I cautiously burned countless pages.
Watched my past slowly fade away
and float into the dust of dark grey.

Sometimes it feels like
I wasted so much time with you.
And I know I won't get back all those days,
but I'm learning that my soul
can search for and rearrange
the hidden galaxies in my mind.

I know that's where I'll find
the beautiful, lost parts that you took from me.

You knocked me off my balance
just like the sky when it breaks its silence.
I let myself get caught in the rain for you.

Sometimes it felt like a lifetime,
but it died in an instant.
And I don't reach inside
my wild mind
for those memories anymore.

The sun finally set for good.
And you're nothing
but an ink blot blur.

I finally started to see things more clear,
the moment I saw his reflection
in the rear-view mirror.
Broken and the same as before.
I've changed.
And I can't ignore,
that you'll never be someone
I search for anymore.

I still felt like I had to be silent.
I was scared I'd lose control.
So, I used my pen to speak instead,
and let my mind connect with my soul.
What started as a way to heal my wounds,
turned into a journey I never knew it could be.

And that was when I realized.
It was poetry.

It was poetry that saved me.

Made in United States
Orlando, FL
29 September 2024